Minnesota Hauntings

Ghost Stories from the Land of 10,000 Lakes

by
Ryan Jacobson

Adventure Publications, Inc.
Cambridge, Minnesota

Dedication:

For my brothers, Jason and Scott.

A special thank you to everyone who willingly shared their ghost stories and who allowed me to put their tales into this collection. I appreciate your time and your patience. I would also like to thank the many people who gave me guidance and who pointed me in the right direction during the process of researching this book.

In some instances, names and locations have been changed at the request of the sources.

Book and cover design by Jonathan Norberg

Edited by Brett Ortler

Page 84 photo copyright Cheri Jacobson

10 9 8 7 6 5 4 3 2 1

Copyright 2010 by Ryan Jacobson
Published by Adventure Publications, Inc.
820 Cleveland Street South
Cambridge, MN 55008
1-800-678-7006
www.adventurepublications.net

ISBN-13: 978-1-59193-301-4
ISBN-10: 1-59193-301-3

Minnesota Hauntings

Ghost Stories from the Land of 10,000 Lakes

Table of Contents

CHILDHOOD CHILLERS

Introduction

BUYER: BEWARE. That's all I can say after the "terrifying tale" my sister-in-law told me. Katie is a huge fan of all things scary, so of course I gave her a copy of my first spooky book, *Ghostly Tales of Wisconsin*.

She brought it to her home outside Princeton, eager to devour its contents. But as she carried the book inside, her dog Lola "freaked out." The pooch glared at *Ghostly Tales*, angrily growling and barking. (Everyone's a critic!) Lola wouldn't stop yipping until Katie shelved the book.

Good ol' Katie saw this as a sign. She immediately devised a theory that a ghost must somehow be attached to it. So when the lights in the vacant house next door started turning on and off at all hours of the night, Katie knew why.

It was the Ghost of the Book.

Eventually, Katie's copy of *Ghostly Tales* vanished. She couldn't remember where she'd left it, and she even began to wonder if her resident spirit had hidden it. But thanks to Lola, Katie solved the mystery a few nights later.

She was awakened by the sound of Lola barking and scratching at the wall beside her bed. The dog had not acted like that since the first time Katie brought home *Ghostly Tales of Wisconsin*.

She turned on the lights—her husband, Mitch, was not pleased—and after a few choice words for Lola, Katie began digging around the floor near the wall. Much to her surprise, she located her missing book. And once again, as soon as Katie put it away, Lola's barking ceased.

Do I subscribe to Katie's Ghost of the Book theory? Not really. (I don't think Katie does either.) But still, I suppose it's plausible. It's enough to make one wonder.

And so it is with most ghost stories. Personally, I think about 90 percent of them are questionable at best. But that still leaves 10 percent as true!

In *Minnesota Hauntings*, I present a balance between the state's best, most famous stories and newly researched ones that have never been published before. I feel it is important to note that, in some instances, I received the details as checklists of unexplainable occurrences rather than as narratives. Thus, while the information remains accurate, some of the scenarios (and characters) were reinterpreted for dramatic effect.

I can neither verify the validity of each claim nor the existence of supernatural beings, but I can assure you that the portrayals of the spirits in this book are as authentic as possible.

And will your copy of *Minnesota Hauntings* come complete with its own ghost? Well, I can give you no promise of that. Enjoy!

Spiteful Spirits

"I have never yet heard of a murderer
who was not afraid of a ghost."

—John Philpot Curran

School Spirit

BISHOP PATRICK R. HEFFRON knelt at the altar. He knew vanity was a sin, but the hardworking man couldn't help feeling proud of his school, Saint Mary's College. He had founded it in Winona three years earlier, and by August 27, 1915, the college had become quite successful. Every aspect of Saint Mary's was running smoothly—at least, everything but the bishop's relationship with Father Louis Lesches.

Heffron recalled his recent communications with the 56-year-old priest. Lesches had demanded a parish of his own, an idea Heffron found almost unimaginable. In truth, the bishop held his colleague in low regard. He wondered about the man's mental stability, and he questioned both his competence and his devotion. The bishop believed Lesches would be more appropriately employed as a farmer, and he'd told him so—a comment that had sent Lesches storming away, mumbling curses under his breath.

"Enough of this," Heffron whispered. He pushed all thoughts of the priest from his mind, reprimanding himself for dwelling on the negative. He focused instead on his prayers.

Thump, thump, thump, thump.

The bishop's concentration was again broken, this time by running footsteps behind him. Heffron stood. He turned to see Father Lesches charging toward him, a frenzied look in his eyes.

"Louis, what are you—" Heffron began to ask. Then he noticed the pistol in Lesches' hand.

Boom! Boom!

The thunderous claps of gunfire echoed through the chapel. Bishop Heffron felt two piercing stabs: the first in his thigh, the second in his chest.

As Lesches hurried away, Heffron found the strength to give chase—but his injuries overcame him. Had Father Thomas Normoyle not discovered the wounded bishop moments later, Heffron may have died.

Instead, by some miracle, the bishop survived to testify against his would-be murderer. He reflected upon the man he had known for more than a decade, describing him as hostile, self-absorbed and friendless. Also noted were the countless arguments between Lesches and another of his colleagues, Father Edward Lynch. In the most heated of moments, Lesches took to screaming a condensed version of the Bible verse, First Thessalonians 4:16. "And the Lord shall come again, to the sound of trumpets!"

The case against Lesches was a slam dunk—it almost certainly would've been even without Heffron's testimony. Police had arrested Lesches mere minutes after the shooting, the gun hidden in the deranged priest's travel bag. However, the murderous man was not put in prison. Instead, he was declared mentally unfit and sent 140 miles west to the Asylum for the Dangerously Insane in Saint Peter.

One might imagine that after Bishop Heffron lost his battle with cancer in 1927, and with Lesches still hospitalized, this bizarre saga would finally reach its conclusion. But the strange tale of Louis Lesches and Saint Mary's College had only just begun.

A Mysterious Death

By January of 1931, Lesches had proven himself to be a model patient. He was declared mentally stable and reportedly would have been freed, if not for a rather significant technicality: Lesches was still under the guardianship of the Diocese of Winona, so the new bishop, Francis Kelley, needed to sign off on Lesches' release. Kelley refused, sending Lesches into a rage.

Perhaps it was coincidence and perhaps not, but on May 15 of that same year, inside Saint Mary's Hall (the building in which Heffron had been shot), nuns discovered one of the most ghastly and puzzling scenes in Minnesota history. Father Lynch, the man whom Lesches had clashed with on so many occasions, was found dead in his third-floor room. His body—or rather his charred remains—lay upon the bed.

Strangely, there was almost no evidence of fire. Lynch's Bible was the only other item burned. Nothing else, not even the bed on which the priest's body rested, was so much as singed.

Even more strangely, while the Good Book lay in ruin, burned almost beyond recognition, a single passage within it was said to have remained untouched, as if the mysterious flames had burned around it. That passage was First Thessalonians 4:16.

Father Lynch's official cause of death was listed as an electrical accident, but many believed that the only viable explanation was a supernatural one. According to legend, Lesches' spirit had claimed its first victim, even though Lesches himself was still among the living, a patient at the state hospital.

The Ghost of Heffron Hall

It wasn't until twelve years later, on January 10, 1943, that the former priest met his end. Lesches passed away from a heart attack at the age of 84, still a resident of the Asylum for the Dangerously Insane.

Almost from the moment of Lesches' death, Saint Mary's Heffron Hall—named after the bishop whom Lesches had tried to kill—reportedly became a hotbed of paranormal activity.

The phenomena began with phantom footsteps heard roaming the third floor, accompanied by the sound of a tapping cane. Several witnesses claimed that the papers on the community bulletin board waved as if caught in a gentle breeze, but there was no source of wind. An invisible presence sometimes kept students from entering the third floor, pushing them back into the stairwell with each effort to cross the threshold. The stories went on and on.

One of the most terrifying encounters on record occurred late one night in 1945. The third-floor hallway's stillness was shattered by the appearance of a shadowy, cloaked figure. The mysterious visitor stood before one of the doors and knocked.

Inside the room, Mike O'Malley and his roommate were awakened by the noise. O'Malley leapt out of bed and flung open the door, surprised to see the figure standing there.

Believing it to be one of the school's priests and trying to comprehend why he'd be at their door at that hour, O'Malley asked, "What do you want, Father?"

The stranger's frightening response was almost a hiss. "I want you!"

The figure moved toward O'Malley, but the student did not back down. He swung his fist hard into the cloaked figure's jaw. Bones snapped, but the visitor was unhurt. Instead, O'Malley suffered substantial injury to his hand, as if he'd hit a brick wall.

With O'Malley writhing in pain, his roommate jumped to his aid. He reached the door and glimpsed the stranger's face just before it vanished. His description of the visitor matched that of Louis Lesches.

The Investigation

Following that frightful encounter, the phenomena in Heffron Hall reportedly grew more intense. Blood flowed from sinks and urinals in the bathroom. Students were chased by an invisible presence, the sound of running feet echoing behind them. And then there were the cold spots . . .

By 1967, tales of the ghost had run so rampant that members of the college's student newspaper, *The Nexus*, organized their own formal investigation. They hoped to debunk the perceived myth, but their results shocked even them.

Setting up in Heffron Hall's third floor hallway, the investigators' evening began rather uneventfully. But at 1:45 a.m.—the time of night Lesches had died 24 years earlier—their equipment detected some bizarre readings: The air temperature dropped significantly at one of their thermometers, and the cold spot began to spread in just one direction, east to west, at a rate of 100 feet in 30 seconds. It was as if an invisible presence were stalking the hallway, leaving a trail of frigid air in its wake.

Furthermore, photos and videos taken by the team were mysteriously blurred and distorted—enough evidence to convince many of the investigators that they had shared a brush with the paranormal.

Most Haunted

The school's eerie phenomena continued throughout the years and decades that followed, and in 1989, *USA Today* declared Saint Mary's College—now Saint Mary's University of Minnesota—the state's "most legendary haunted place."

It is a reputation that holds firm, even today, as many believe the ghost of Louis Lesches still roams the floors of Heffron Hall, haunting the building named after a man whom he hated enough to shoot.

Phantom Lady

THE DOG SENSED IT immediately. That's what Anne Kuznar first remembered about the haunting, which lasted more than 12 years. In 1996, she and her then-fiancé Robert Baer moved into an old cabin-turned-house outside the east-central city of Cambridge. The peculiar happenings began almost at once.

"What's Yukon doing?" Anne asked as she entered the living room.

Robert, who had been observing the pet for several minutes, shrugged. "I don't know."

The dog was a wolf-shepherd mix, and he seemed

enamored with something in the far corner—a corner that appeared to be entirely empty. He paced back and forth, sniffing the air. Then Yukon sat, staring upward at the wall, whimpering softly. After a moment's hesitation, the dog stood on all four paws and repeated the ritual. Again. And again.

It was only after Anne called the animal to her side that he ceased his peculiar pattern. But it wasn't the last time he acted in such a manner. Over the next several months, Robert and Anne frequently caught Yukon sitting at the corner, glaring at something only he could see. (Bizarrely, years later, the Baers' next wolf-shepherd dog, Grizzly, did the very same thing.)

During those same months, Anne also began to notice other strange phenomena. From time to time, she would walk through a spot so cold that it caused her to shudder, even on the hottest of summer days (and without an air conditioner to blame for it). Unexplained noises echoed throughout the house, and small objects became "lost," only to be found days later in the oddest of places.

Perhaps most alarming was the disappearance of Anne and Robert's marriage license shortly after they received it. The happy couple had been planning to wed on August 17, 1996, but they could not do so without their license. They spent endless, panicked days searching every inch of their home for that vital piece of paper. It was nowhere to be found; Anne and Robert postponed the wedding until a new license could be issued.

Even after they exchanged their vows, the Baers' paranormal problems continued. In fact, the ghostly encounters grew more dramatic. One night, while Anne was lying on the couch watching television, a blur of movement caught her eye. She looked toward a window, which clearly reflected the room behind her, and she was startled to spy an unfamiliar woman standing beside the couch. Anne turned from the reflection and toward the spot where a stranger should have been. Surprisingly, no one was there.

A few weeks later, Robert awakened in the middle of the night to the scare of his life: The ghostly figure of a woman stood at the foot of his bed! He tried to sit up; he tried to raise his arms and legs—he couldn't move. Robert was paralyzed. He couldn't even call for help. He felt as if heavy weights were pressing against every inch of his body.

The frightening sensation lasted less than a minute, but to Robert it seemed an eternity. At last, the specter faded away, and Robert was free to move again. He did not return to sleep that night.

Sparked by their uniquely disturbing encounters, the Baers began investigating the history of their property. While their research provided no real leads, Robert and Anne came to believe that a woman must have lost her life on their land before it was homesteaded.

Believing the ghost had done its worst, the couple chose not to sell their home. But they did redecorate. Together, Anne and Robert lifted their large, heavy TV off the trunk it had rested on since they first came into the home. Next, they prepared to move the empty old trunk. On a whim, Anne flipped it open and peeked inside. There, at the bottom of the trunk, sat a lone piece of paper: the missing marriage license.

Murderous Intent

THE TROUBLE STARTED in 1986, the year the renovations began. It was the year they removed the false ceiling inside Saint Paul's historic Fitzgerald Theater, discovering an additional balcony—and a note that was addressed to an old stagehand, Ben. Most believed the latter discovery awakened the deceased employee's spirit, and for some reason, Ben's ghost wasn't happy.

Andy Wolter couldn't help but reflect on this as he and his coworker, Tom, carefully stepped into the work area backstage. A narrow flashlight beam was all they had to guide them through their dark surroundings.

Andy admired the Fitzgerald Theater's rich history. Built in 1910, the World Theater (as it was called in the 1980s) was Saint Paul's oldest remaining theater. It was perhaps best known as the site of Garrison Keillor's radio program, *A Prairie Home Companion*, since 1981. But right now, in the darkness, the only thing on Andy's mind was Ben. Andy noticed Tom's flashlight shaking ever so slightly, and he wondered if his coworker was experiencing similar thoughts.

There had been rumors of a dark, shadowy figure roaming the premises—a figure that many witnesses claimed had faded in and out of existence before their eyes. Plus, an antique bottle of muscatel repeatedly disappeared, only to turn up hours (or sometimes days) later in the most unlikely of places.

Andy, himself, had experienced similar phenomena: His work tools kept moving to spots where he knew they shouldn't be. The man had also walked through several of the random cold spots that so many others complained about. And, of course, even Andy knew that unexplained cold spots in the middle of otherwise warm areas were signs of a haunting.

"Let's get this done and get out of here," Tom said.

Andy nodded, even though his colleague couldn't see him. Together, they continued forward.

Whoosh! Andy felt a sudden, forceful wind against his face. It was followed by a thunderous *clap!* Something large and heavy had passed inches from where he stood, landing directly between the two of them.

"What was that?" Tom exclaimed.

"I don't know," answered Andy. "Something fell."

Tom spun and shone his flashlight at the object. A sizeable chunk of ceiling plaster lay crumbled and broken at their feet. Andy gasped, realizing with horror that he had been one step away from certain death.

Tom aimed his flashlight upward. Instinctively, Andy's gaze followed. He wasn't sure what he expected to see—a gaping hole in the ceiling, perhaps—but what he witnessed instead haunted him for years to come. On the catwalk more than sixty feet above him, the light's beam illuminated the outline of a hazy, dark figure.

For the briefest of moments, Andy contemplated the almost unfathomable idea that a person had tried to kill him. But then the mysterious shape disappeared, fading into nothingness like a cloud of mist. It hadn't been a person at all.

"Did you see that?" yelped Tom.

Andy nodded again. "Yeah, but I don't believe it."

The two men turned once more to the chunk of plaster between them.

"Did that thing really just try to murder us?" said Tom, his voice quivering.

"Maybe it was a coincidence," Andy replied. "Maybe a ceiling piece randomly broke and fell."

Tom bent down, examining the debris more closely. After a moment's pause, he turned his gaze toward Andy, shaking his head.

"It can't be," said Tom. "This is plaster."

Andy stared back at him, quizzically. "So?"

Tom shone his flashlight upward once more. "The ceiling—it isn't made of plaster," he declared. "This piece came from nowhere."

Both men hurried out of the backstage area. They refused to work there, in the dark, ever again.

Deadman's Hill

HE HAD MADE IT as far as Minnesota—a farm outside Willmar to be exact. The escaped slave, "Marcus," had been on the run for weeks, perhaps months, but he was out of places to hide. A bounty hunter had caught up with him at last.

Ever since Congress passed the Fugitive Slave Act in 1850, escaping to the North was not enough. Bounty hunters were allowed to pursue runaways all the way to the Canadian border, to capture them and to return them to their "masters." Marcus dreamed of living the rest of his life as a free man in Canada, but his greatest hopes were on the verge of being dashed. He was beaten and bloodied, his foot chained to a fence post. However, he wasn't about to give up. Marcus would either live as a free man or die trying.

He patiently waited, well into the night, until he felt certain that the bounty hunter was asleep. When the time was right, Marcus sprang into action. Summoning his remaining strength, he quietly struggled against the thick, wooden post—pulling, pushing and lifting. It loosened. Marcus strained even harder. At last, the post came out of the ground.

The runaway tasted freedom once more. He began to flee, dragging the heavy post behind him. But luck worked against the unfortunate man. The clanging of his chains awakened the bounty hunter; Marcus's last, desperate flight was stalled.

This time, he refused to surrender; he fought back. A terrible struggle ensued. Marcus may have stood a fighting chance, if not for the chain that confined him—and if not for his captor's sword. The escaped slave was mortally wounded in the battle. But before he died, Marcus turned the weapon against its owner, striking the bounty hunter with a fatal blow to the head.

The next morning, the farmer who owned the land opened his front door to the surprise of his life. "Lord have mercy," he cried. "Ellen, get out here!"

Marcus's lifeless body, still chained to the post, lay sprawled near the front porch. Behind him, a crimson-stained trail led to the top of the nearby hill.

The farmer and his wife cautiously followed the bloody trail. At the end of it, they came upon the dead bounty hunter. They buried him there, dubbing the site Deadman's Hill. The family also dug a grave beside their home for Marcus, planting an American Elm to commemorate the spot. But while Marcus's body was laid to rest, his spirit thirsted for vengeance.

"Honey, have you found my gloves yet?" the farmer complained. "It's been three days."

"I've looked everywhere," his wife replied. "They're not here. Did you check the barn?"

"Yes, and I can't—" He stopped suddenly, staring at his missing gloves, neatly stacked atop the kitchen table.

"Where in the world did these come from?" the farmer muttered. "They weren't here a second ago."

Mysteriously, the gloves became the first of many items to disappear from the house, only to turn up days later in strange locations or in places that had already been checked.

One night, as darkness descended upon the Willmar farmland, the family's situation grew much worse. The hard-working couple lay in bed, ready for sleep, when they noticed a faint echo in the distance.

"Do you hear that?" the farmer asked.

"Yes," his wife whispered nervously.

Upon first listen, the noise was indistinguishable. But slowly and steadily it grew louder—as if its source were drawing closer.

The terrifying noise became two distinctly separate sounds. With a sudden, chilling horror, the farmer recognized them: the dreadful moans and the rattling chains of a ghost; it was approaching from the top of Deadman's Hill.

Against his better judgment, the farmer leapt to the window. But the instant he gazed outside, toward the now-notorious hill, the frightful noises ceased. Nothing—and no one—was there.

That alone would be enough to scare away even the bravest, most resolute of people. However, this was far from the worst that Marcus's spirit had planned. It was out for blood.

Years later, during an especially snowy winter, the phantom returned again. A sharecropper working the land disappeared. A search party gathered to locate him, but they found much more than they bargained for.

"Help, I need help!" one of the volunteers shouted. "Up on the hill. I— I— I think I found him."

The others gathered with the man atop Deadman's Hill. Together, they stared in stunned silence at the savaged remains of their missing neighbor. He had been brutally murdered, his head nearly chopped off.

Similarly, a hired hand was later killed in almost exactly the same spot. In both instances, the only clue left behind was a trail in the snow. It was as if the murderer had appeared out of thin air and had dragged something large and heavy away from each victim—before disappearing at the bottom of the hill.

Today, Deadman's Hill remains one of the most notorious haunted spots in the state. While no other victims have been reported, few people dare to venture onto the haunted hill alone—fearing that Marcus's spirit may once again re-enact the battle that took his life more than 150 years ago.

Haunted Homes

"An idea, like a ghost, must be spoken
to a little before it will explain itself."

–Charles Dickens

New House Nightmare

THE HOME WAS BEAUTIFUL, the location even better. Newly constructed and safely tucked within a private, secluded cul de sac, it was everything Mike and Ashley Howe wanted their place to be. They eagerly purchased it and moved into the Lakeville home, south of the Twin Cities, in August of 2005. Neither thought twice about the adjacent cemetery—at least, not until it was too late.

The Howes' first day as homeowners was long, tedious and hot. They spent the morning with pens in hand, tackling an almost endless stack of papers and official documents. The couple then labored, through-out the afternoon and well into the evening, carrying furniture and countless boxes into their new house. By eight o'clock, the arduous task of unpacking had begun, and by midnight, the exhausted couple was in bed.

Both believed that sleep would come easily, and both slowly drifted out of consciousness, their eyes closed, memories of the day fading, fading, fading.

Crash!

A loud noise rang from the basement. The thun-derous clang rattled the bedroom windows. The couple's dogs barked ferociously. Ashley and Mike bolted upright in bed.

"What was that?" the woman exclaimed.

Mike stared at her wide-eyed. "It sounded like something tipped over below us. Only louder."

He jumped out of bed, and he rummaged around the room, searching for anything that might pass as a weapon. He decided upon a small wooden lamp, clutch-ing it tightly like a club.

Mike snuck out of the bedroom and cautiously crept downstairs. He searched the entire basement, room after room. He found exactly what he expected: nothing. The Howes hadn't yet moved anything into the lower level; the basement was completely empty.

That first bizarre occurrence might possibly have been rationalized, explained away or even forgotten, except it was only the beginning. The dogs began acting up—running around the house and barking wildly—at all hours and for no apparent reason. The bedroom lights inexplicably flickered on and off. And in two separate instances, Ashley heard an eerie, distant voice calling her name when she was alone.

On a particularly sleepy Saturday morning, Ashley was awakened when her husband's alarm clock buzzed to life. While Mike rose out of bed and groggily staggered into the bathroom, Ashley thanked her luck that she wasn't the one scheduled to work.

She rolled onto her side, facing the wall, with every intention of returning to sleep. Much to her surprise, Mike rejoined her. She felt him snuggle up beside her and wrap his arm around her waist. Ashley loved when he did that; Mike's thick, rugged arms were like armor against the dangers of the world.

"I thought you had to work," she whispered. She touched his forearm and stroked it gently. It was thin and smooth . . .

. . . and not at all like Mike's!

Ashley's eyes flew open. She leapt out of bed. She turned to face the stranger, not daring to imagine whom she might see. To her horror and relief, she found no one else there.

Unfortunately for the Howes, a housing market crash left them trapped in a home they believed to be haunted. But the spirit did no worse. For the most part, it seemed content to flicker a few lights and to make strange noises. Hopefully, it will always stay that way.

Poltergeist

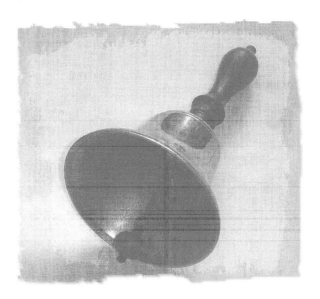

IT BEGAN AS a gray something. Rachel was seven years old, giddy with excitement as she explored her family's new farmhouse, nestled along Highway 47, west of Cambridge. Built at the turn of the century, the east-central Minnesota home was now 69 years old—and if it had a tragic history, the Hartmans were unaware of it.

Rachel skipped up the stairs, heading to her bedroom. Her family had lived in the house for less than a week, so every trip up and down the steps still felt like a new adventure. As Rachel hurried onward, daydreaming about ponies and princesses, she suddenly stopped in her tracks. Something was on the stairs with her—something she'd never seen before.

Rachel felt a chill as a gray, cloudlike shape breezed toward her. The seven-year-old slipped sideways; it passed directly beside her. She spun to watch the gray thing continue its descent, but it was no longer there.

This marked the first and only time Rachel ever physically encountered the apparition, but it was just the beginning of the ghostly happenings in store for her—and for her sister, Pam.

As Rachel grew older, her bedroom seemed to be the favorite target of whatever invisible force resided within the Hartmans' home. Fortunately for her, the ghost contented itself on playing with her bedroom's doors. Rachel's closet and crawl space entrances opened without cause on far too many occasions to count, never stopping from the time her family moved into the house until the day Rachel left for college.

New Owners

In 1977, Rachel's father tragically passed away, and the question soon arose: what to do with the farmhouse? The solution came from Pam. Recently married to Ross Mauer and with a young child, her new family bought the house in 1981.

The Mauers' dog, Cinder, was their first indication that the ghost was still present. An "inside dog" all of his life, the pooch was suddenly willing to do anything and everything to get outdoors. Pam and Ross couldn't leave a downstairs window open, or Cinder would jump through the screen. (One time, he even leapt through the glass, resulting in a trip to the veterinarian!)

Their pet's new behavior was curious, but Pam soon learned why her dog was so frightened. The spirit, which had been little more than an afterthought throughout most of her childhood, was about to turn this haunting up a notch.

Perhaps serving as a precursor to the terrifying events that would follow, the Mauers were visited by two 80-year-old women shortly after moving into their home.

"We lived here as children," said one of the visitors. "Do you mind if we look around for old time's sake?"

Pam welcomed the women inside and showed them around the house before treating them to a cup of tea.

"There were fifteen of us kids, although six died in infancy. We were a big family," said the woman.

"But then there was the incident," noted the other.

"Yes, two of the children were twins." The first's voice dropped to whisper. "One of them accidentally shot and killed the other, right here inside the house."

Pam grimaced. Their story offered a possible origin for the home's paranormal presence—and to tell the truth, it was more than she wanted to know.

Bed Times

During the years that followed, the phantom seemed to target Pam—and only Pam. The woman's bedroom doors mysteriously opened and closed, just as they had done for Rachel throughout her childhood. But now, on top of that, the bed she shared with Ross inexplicably began shaking uncontrollably, awakening them in the middle of almost every night.

Pam frequently felt peculiar, cool breezes blowing against her inside the house. She heard footsteps on the second floor while she was home alone. And on a few occasions, she sensed someone sitting beside her on the living room couch and on her bed. But when she looked, no one else was there.

Throughout the ordeal, Pam took solace in the fact that she remained the ghost's main victim—and not her children. The protective mother guarded her daughter and son against all knowledge of the poltergeist. But in 1987, when Lisa was 12 years old, even that changed.

"Mom," Lisa confessed, "something weird has been happening to me."

Pam's interest was immediately piqued. She prayed her daughter wasn't going to say . . .

"Sometimes, at night, when I'm trying to sleep, my whole bed starts shaking," Lisa told her mother.

Pam sighed. It was time for full disclosure.

Through the course of her conversation with Lisa, Pam heard a story that was eerily similar to Rachel's first encounter, nearly 20 years earlier. Lisa had been lying on her bed one morning, when she noticed a white cloud floating over her. She watched as it glided through her room, into the hallway and down the stairs, where she lost sight of it.

The chilling account was a confirmation of Pam's worst fears. The ghost had a new target: her daughter.

Sights and Sounds

True enough, the spirit began terrorizing both of the Mauer females—most often with the same stunts it had used for decades. However, the poltergeist had a few new tricks, as well.

Pam was in the kitchen when she heard the soft tinkle of a handbell, ringing in the adjacent living room. She kept such a bell on a shelf in there, but it was only for decoration. She couldn't imagine why Lisa would be fooling around with it.

The bell rang again. Maybe this was Lisa's idea of a joke: summoning her mom to cater to her every whim.

"What?" Pam called into the living room.

No answer.

"If you need something, you're going to have to tell me," Pam sang.

The bell rang once more, and Pam rolled her eyes, admitting defeat. She trudged into the living room. "Okay, what do you want?"

The room was empty. The bell sat on its shelf, as if it had never been moved.

Lisa, too, had a frightful living room encounter. She was seventeen at the time, and she'd just sent her friends home. It was late, almost midnight, and the teenaged girl believed her parents were both upstairs asleep—until her mother called from the living room. "Lisa."

The girl found it strange that her mom would be in there with the lights off. She stepped into the darkness, but she did not find her mother. Instead, she saw two floating arms reaching out from nowhere. They motioned as if to set something down on an invisible table.

Lisa bolted out of the living room and retreated upstairs to find her parents. She never felt more eager to graduate from high school and to get out of that house.

The Final Encounter

Pam could live with opening doors and bumps in the night, but this haunting had become too sinister—and the worst was yet to come. The woman experienced something so terrifying that she felt compelled to write about it the very next day.

What follows is Pam's final ghostly encounter, as described in her own words:

"Last night I couldn't sleep. It was 1:30 when I finally drifted off but slept restlessly, waking and sleeping. At 4:00 I went downstairs to go to the bathroom. I came back up and laid down with [my son]. I was just drifting off again when he woke up whimpering and talking. I laid him back down and looked toward the end of the bed. There is a night light in the bedroom, so it wasn't completely dark.

"There, by our legs, was a torso of a young man—no head or legs I could see, just a white, transparent-looking shirt with a body in it. The shirt was of the older days, like a fancy tuxedo shirt.

"I said, 'Get out of here,' and tried to push it away.

"My hand went through the torso—that's when I jumped out of bed and ran to the hall and turned on the light, thinking to myself, *That's enough. I'm getting out of this house.*

"I immediately came back in the room. The torso was gone. Needless to say, I slept with the hall light on the rest of the night."

Almost immediately after documenting this account, Pam and her family began packing. They moved out of their home a few days later. The property was eventually sold and the old farmhouse torn down. It marked the conclusion of a haunting that had lasted nearly 30 years.

The Haunted Hutch

"SURPRISE!" exclaimed Lila Palmer.

Her daughter Jenny stifled a gasp. It was indeed a surprise—but not a good one. Jenny's parents had unexpectedly arrived at her Thief River Falls home. And while they were always welcome to visit, the gift they had brought was not a happy sight.

The china hutch was a gorgeous piece of furniture, but its worth was measured only in sentimental value. The antique had been passed down from mother to daughter for generations. Apparently, now it was Jenny's turn to own it.

As a child, Jenny had never given much thought to the hutch. She would have ignored it all together if not for the times she had gotten into trouble on its behalf. The items displayed behind the hutch's glass doors had a strange habit of rearranging themselves, and the hutch doors often popped open without explanation.

For years, Jenny shouldered the blame, even though she was innocent. Fortunately for her, when she was eight years old, her mother witnessed a door opening on its own; a statuette jumped off its shelf and onto the floor. After that, Jenny wasn't blamed anymore.

Before the girl's ninth birthday, the Palmers hit a stretch of bad luck. The family's house was burglarized, and the thieves took several hunting rifles and a jewelry collection that included Lila's heirloom wedding rings.

Mere months later, an electrical fire destroyed the Palmer's home, consuming most of their belongings. The only item to survive the blaze was the old hutch. Lila took special care in cleaning the soot off her prized possession, and while she did so, she made a startling discovery: The two stolen wedding rings had suddenly appeared on one of the hutch's shelves.

Even after the Palmers moved the hutch into their new home, its contents continued to change positions, and the doors sometimes opened themselves. At first, these happenings were little more than fun conversation topics. However, as the years passed, Jenny detected a ghastly pattern: Every time the hutch doors opened, a loved one died within three months!

Jenny hated herself for discovering the correlation. She spent most of her teen years in fear of finding the hutch open, and when this harbinger came, she waited in dreadful anticipation for death to find someone she cared about. It always did, without exception.

By contrast, in the years after she left the hutch behind, Jenny didn't attend a single funeral. It would seem that in escaping the antique cabinet, she had saved her family and friends from the Grim Reaper.

Yet here it was. Death—the hutch—had found her again. Jenny silently debated her options. Although it would break her mother's heart, she eventually chose to refuse the gift. She didn't have to.

As the hutch was lifted off the truck, the glass on its doors broke. Jenny tried not to smile; now she had an excuse for keeping it in the garage.

Three years came and went, and the hutch sat in storage. But time softened Jenny's opinion of the family treasure. Eventually her sentiments got the better of her. (The hutch's predictions of death couldn't be real. They were simply matters of coincidence.) She fixed the hutch and moved it into her dining room.

For the better part of a month, Jenny enjoyed the old piece of furniture without incident. Then one day it happened. Jenny came home from grocery shopping to find the hutch's doors standing open.

Exactly three months later, her 36-year-old cousin died from a heart attack. Jenny wasted no time in getting rid of the hutch, once and for all.

Eternal Love

PERHAPS SHE'D SEEN too many romance films or had read too many Jane Austen novels, but Joleen "JoJo" Jones dreamed of being swept off her feet. That did not necessarily mean wild adventures, tropical vacations or grand gestures of affection. JoJo believed it was the little things that built a lasting love. A morning kiss goodbye, quiet dinners together and, of course, those tiny favors which would make a spouse's life just a touch easier—that was JoJo's definition of love.

She liked to blame her favorite childhood stories, such as *Cinderella* and *The Little Mermaid*, but regardless of the reason, JoJo had been desperately seeking her one true love since she'd first started dating. Now, eight years later, she was fresh from college and carving a "grown-up" life for herself. She had a boyfriend (although she was not yet sure if he were the one). She'd found a job in the west-central Minnesota town of Morris, and she had rented an old farmhouse outside the city limits.

Even on her first day, when she moved her truck-load of belongings into the old place, JoJo felt uneasy. Every trip inside brought feelings of loneliness, heart-break and dread. More than once, the young woman considered changing her mind, putting everything back into the truck and driving home with her mom and dad. But logic won the day, and JoJo decided that she was being silly. This was, after all, a landmark moment in her life. The "off" feeling was probably just nervousness. Wasn't it?

The following morning, JoJo awoke to find her back door light switched on. While she believed she'd turned it off before bed, the discovery barely registered as odd. So too, on her second morning inside the house, JoJo didn't think much about finding the same light on again. But she wasn't about to make that mistake for a third night in a row. At 10:15 p.m., just before bed, JoJo specifically checked the light, ensuring that it was off.

The next day, the back door light was on!

For a moment, panic swelled within her. She recalled her strange feelings upon moving into the house. But JoJo quickly dismissed her worries. She felt certain that there were any number of reasonable explanations for the phenomenon.

During her lunch break, she telephoned Randy and told him about the light. The dutiful boyfriend eased her mind. Something of a fix-it man, Randy assured JoJo that the switch was probably on a timer, and he promised to look at it when he visited over the weekend.

JoJo breathed a sigh of relief.

Still, she made certain the light was off before going to bed both that night and the next. However, she was not surprised to find it flipped on each morning. It was simply due to the timer.

Friday night arrived, and with it came Randy. The young woman was so excited to see her boyfriend's familiar face that she forgot all about the back door light. It wasn't until the next morning, when she again discovered it flipped on, that she remembered.

JoJo asked Randy to take a look at it, but when he did, he was immediately puzzled. "There's no timer on here," he said. "You'd be able to see it."

"How is that possible?" asked JoJo.

"I don't know. But as long as I'm looking, let's take it apart. Maybe we can figure it out."

For the next twenty minutes Randy tooled around with the mysterious switch. He found nothing wrong, not even a hint as to how the light was turning on every single night.

JoJo's fears returned, but Randy quickly tempered them. A perfectly reasonable explanation was out there, probably. But even if it weren't, so what? This was just a light switch—no big deal.

That night, at just after 10:30 p.m., the couple sat in the living room together. Suddenly, they heard a *click*. The light switch had just been flipped. JoJo leapt from her chair and dashed to the back door; Randy followed. Neither was surprised to find the light now on, but this time they'd heard it happen.

On Sunday night, Randy returned to college. JoJo once again found herself alone with her fears, an ordeal that proved difficult to handle. She grew paranoid, she had trouble sleeping, and she began to consider moving. Unfortunately, her financial situation was fragile. She could not afford to break her lease. Plus, the rent was cheap. (Now she knew why!)

As the weeks progressed, JoJo's fears were slowly replaced by curiosity. She fell into the habit of sitting by that back door every night, at just after 10:30 p.m. Sure enough, every night, the switch would flip on before her eyes. She wanted to know more, to discover exactly what was happening. She even asked her landlord, but he claimed ignorance, promising to look into the "electrical glitch." But then one day a story came to her. Perhaps it was a coping mechanism, or perhaps the house's ghost granted her this knowledge; JoJo wasn't sure which. Either way, it was a tale that she would never forget:

Thomas Peters lived in that old farmhouse his entire life, and when he married Lillian Polaschek in 1946, they took over the place together. Sadly, a 1972 accident left the man unable to work the land, so he was forced to find a job in town. He took the best position he could get: the second shift at a local factory.

For nearly thirty years he worked there, returning home just after 11 p.m. each night. Lillian, meanwhile, tended to the house. And it was with much love that she fell into the habit of turning on that back door light for her husband—night after night, year after year, decade after decade. It became her routine to watch the ten o'clock news, get ready for bed, turn on the light and wait for Thomas. When he arrived, she always greeted him with a kiss.

Sadly, time took its toll. In 1999, Lillian passed away at the age of 71. However, it would seem that even the grave couldn't diminish her love. Not even death kept her from performing that office for her beloved husband. Thomas worked at the factory for two more years (until he too passed away), and every night when he returned home, he found the back door light switched on.

For Lillian Peters, love was the back door light, her special favor to the man she cherished, the light that led him through the darkness, ensuring that he returned to her safely.

As for JoJo, this tale of eternal love impacted her profoundly. She realized that Randy was not a man for whom she'd turn on a light each and every night, so she ended their romantic relationship. She stayed in that old house for two more years, until a career change led her to other parts of the state.

Eventually JoJo did find her "Thomas." She is now happily married, and she looks forward to expanding her family. Perhaps their love will prove to be as timeless as that of Thomas and Lillian Peters.

Relative-ly Haunted

"I figure I basically am a ghost. I think we all are."

—John Astin

Grandma Ghost

HE WASN'T ALONE. Someone—or something— was there with him. At least, that's how James Jensen felt whenever he entered his house's second-floor, southwest bedroom. He'd moved into the Albert Lea home with his family in 1893, proud to have constructed it with his own hands. Unfortunately, the housewarming was spoiled shortly thereafter, when Jensen's grandmother died on the premises.

Now, as goose bumps formed on the back of his neck, Jensen couldn't help but remember his deceased relative. "Hello," he called. "Is anybody there?"

No one answered. No one ever did. But Jensen grew convinced of a supernatural house guest, and he wasn't the only one. None of his family members ever dared to use that bedroom.

The ghost must not have been too bothersome, though. Despite all of the eerie feelings, creepy noises and unexplained occurrences, the Jensens stayed with their house—and its spirit—for more than 50 years. They finally sold the place in 1946.

Many believed that the Jensens' departure angered the resident phantom, for the paranormal presence that had remained barely perceptible for over five decades suddenly morphed into a terrifying force. It drove away the next thirteen homeowners in a span of fourteen years. By 1960, the property had run out of takers. It was abandoned and left to rot.

When Dick and Anita Borland purchased the vacant house in 1964, it was something of a "fixer upper." Nevertheless, the Borlands were determined to make a go of it, believing that their family of eleven was up to the task of renovating.

Even before they moved in, the Borlands set out to make the place more presentable.

"It's a nice day," Anita noted, "perfect for cleaning the front yard."

Her family went to work, but one of the helping relatives soon disrupted the morning duties.

"Who's that?" she cried, pointing toward the house.

The others followed her gesture with their eyes, gazing toward the southwest bedroom. They spied an elderly woman standing on the upstairs porch.

Not recognizing her and unable to get her attention, the Borlands dashed inside the house. They hurried upstairs, but by the time they reached the porch, the old woman had vanished.

The coming months brought more bizarre sightings. Most family members encountered the old woman's specter a time or two—especially near the closet in the southwest bedroom. Often the apparition would appear, floating outside the door. Then it would turn and charge into the closet, vanishing from view.

On one dark, rainy afternoon, two of the Borland children—Rebecca and Richard—raced up the steps and into the hallway. With their chores finished, they were eager for an opportunity to play in their rooms.

They didn't make it.

A strange, lanky woman appeared before them. She wore a white apron over a flowery dress, her expression a mixture of frustration and terror. She seemed frantic, desperately searching for something she needed.

The children stared at her, frozen with fear, mouths hanging open.

Suddenly, as if finally realizing that she wasn't alone, the specter turned toward Rebecca and Richard. "Help me," she pleaded. "Please, help me!" Her voice sounded distant and cold.

The Borland siblings turned and ran downstairs. By the time they retrieved their mother and returned to the second-floor hallway, the apparition was gone.

This encounter and those that followed led Anita to dig into the house's history. She interviewed a relative of the original homeowners and learned about Grandma Jensen. The discovery seemed to put the Borlands—and their ghost—at ease. The family remained at their home for years. No major encounters were ever again reported.

Cameryn

LEA FRITZ FELT A TWINGE of panic as she searched the Ely home in northeastern Minnesota. It was early; her two-year-old-daughter, Cameryn, should still be asleep. But when Lea had peeked inside her youngest child's room, she had found Cameryn's bed empty. Now, the nervous woman hurried from bathroom to living room to kitchen—her mind conjuring any number of parental nightmares.

Lea dashed into her oldest daughter Jordan's room, and her heart nearly stopped. Cameryn lay face down on the floor, unconscious and eerily still. The frantic mother dove to her daughter's side, noticing a nearby outlet and fearing that Cameryn had been electrocuted. She cradled her child and felt with increasing alarm that the two-year-old was cold to the touch.

"Cameryn," she pleaded. "Wake up!"

The girl's eyes fluttered, then opened. Lea squeezed her daughter tightly. "Cameryn, you scared me half to death. What are you doing in here?"

"She came to play. She wanted to see Jordan too," Cameryn confessed. "I took her here, and I fell asleep. Is she gone?"

"Who?" asked Lea, believing that her daughter had been dreaming.

A shy smile brushed across the girl's face. She softly giggled. "Grandma Ag."

Lea was startled by the reference to her own grand-mother, but she quickly shrugged it off. Agnes passed away more than nine years earlier, so Cameryn had never met her. But certainly Lea had mentioned Grandma Ag once or twice in passing. The child was just fantasizing about a relative she would never know.

At least, that's what Lea believed.

The following days brought more reported visits. Cameryn revealed several interesting details about her great-grandmother—details the two-year-old could not possibly have known. Cameryn noted how Grandma always wore a dress and that Grandma loved to garden. She even mentioned that Grandma Ag didn't like fake flowers—all of which Lea knew to be true.

One afternoon, while Lea watched Cameryn play on the backyard swing set, she noticed one of the empty swings start to move. Cameryn looked toward it and laughed playfully.

"Is someone with you?" Lea asked.

"Just Grandma Ag," came the response.

On a whim, Lea decided to dig out an old photo album and share it with her daughter. As they paged through the pictures, Cameryn suddenly smiled and exclaimed, "Mommy, there she is. There's Grandma Ag."

Indeed, it was. And in that moment, Lea became convinced that her grandmother's ghost was visiting the house each night.

By Cameryn's account, she enjoyed Grandma Ag's company. "We read books, and she always tells me to be good," said the child.

Lea felt warmed to hear it. She had been close to her grandma, and the sentiment sounded like something Grandma Ag would say.

"The next time you see her," whispered Lea, "will you tell her I miss her?"

Cameryn shrugged and said, "She knows, Mommy. She misses you, too."

Grumpy Ghosts

Unfortunately, not every ghostly visit was blissful. Soon, Cameryn began talking about other spirits. She told her mother that she'd met Papa Ag and didn't like him; he was grouchy. True enough, Lea's grandfather (who had died while Lea was in high school) had been something of a sourpuss while alive.

Cameryn also shared stories of a baby who would come to eat in her room—but only if the bedroom door were closed. Whenever Cameryn saw the tiny specter, she would rush to her room, close the door and remain in there until the baby was finished.

On a drive home from the grocery store, Cameryn startled her mother when she asked, "Who's that man?"

"What man?" Lea replied.

Cameryn pointed out the window and said in an alarmingly casual manner, "The man right there. He came out of the ground. He's flying by the truck."

Lea turned to look, but as she did, her daughter said, "Oh, he's gone now."

Another of Cameryn's ghosts was a little boy named Marty. Lea learned about him at the kitchen table one night, while the family was eating dinner.

"Marty's here," Cameryn announced suddenly. Her face had lost a bit of its color.

"Who's Marty?" asked Lea.

"He's mean, Mommy. I don't like him. Make him go away."

"Why don't you like him, Sweetie? What makes him mean?"

Cameryn squinted and then blinked hard, as if she were fighting back tears. "He's weird, and he wants me to play bad games. Sometimes he wears a dress when I see him. Can you please make him go away?"

"Where is Marty now?"

Her daughter pointed toward the adjacent steps. Lea stood and walked to them, wondering if she might encounter a cold spot or experience an eerie feeling. She felt nothing. Lea waved her hands blindly and asked, "Is he here? Am I close?"

"Mommy, stop it!" Cameryn screamed. "You're touching him!"

Lea returned to the table and calmed her daughter. "Have you tried asking Marty to leave you alone?"

"I can't Mommy. I'm scared. You tell him."

"Since I can't see Marty, he probably won't listen to me." She lovingly squeezed her daughter's shoulder. "It'll have to come from you. Tell him that he doesn't live here, and if he sees any kind of light, he needs to go to it."

Despite Lea's strongest assurances, Cameryn refused. The idea of talking to Marty terrified her. Nevertheless, perhaps Marty's spirit overheard Lea's advice. It was not seen again.

In fact, all of Cameryn's ghostly sightings tapered off after that night. Within a matter of months, the little girl's supernatural visitors were a distant memory—an almost forgotten phase of youth, slipping from her mind like so much of our early childhood tends to do.

A Cemetery Visit

During the summer after Cameryn's sixth birthday, the child surprised her mother by asking a strange and unexpected question. "Where does Grandma Ag live?"

"She lives in heaven," replied Lea.

The girl shook her head. "No, where is she now?"

Lea looked at her daughter intently. "Do you mean where is she buried?"

Cameryn nodded.

"At the cemetery in Tower. Do you think you want to go see her?"

The girl clapped and squealed with glee. "I do!"

So it was on Saturday afternoon in August that Lea, Jordan and Cameryn went to visit Grandma Ag's grave. Cameryn brought a flower and laid it beside the tombstone. Then the girl pointed at two beautiful—albeit weathered and faded—bouquets, also resting next to the grave. "Grandma wants us to move those," Cameryn said resolutely.

Puzzled, Lea bent down, scooped up both bouquets and examined them closely. The flowers were fake.

The Ghost of Glensheen

AS A TOUR GUIDE of Duluth's Glensheen, the Historic Congdon Estate, Tracy Benson knew the ins and outs of the mansion. It was her job. She also knew all about the home's grisly past—even if the details were rarely discussed with visitors to the landmark North Shore locale.

The glorious home was built between 1905 and 1908 by one of Duluth's richest residents, Chester Congdon. He was a respected businessman and politician, and his 39-room mansion on London Road became the talk of the town, recognized as an architectural masterpiece.

However, on June 26, 1977, the spotlight shone on Glensheen Mansion for a different reason: It became the site of one of the most notorious crimes in Minnesota's history. Congdon's daughter Elisabeth, now 83 years old, was murdered in her bed. Her night nurse, Velma Pietila was killed as well.

Police quickly reconstructed the tragic crimes. A burglar broke into the mansion through a basement window on the night of June 26. The criminal crept up the stairwell, where he ran into Pietila by chance. The unfortunate encounter spelled doom for the night nurse, as the surprised intruder panicked. He brutally bludgeoned Pietila to death with a brass candlestick.

The vicious murderer wasn't finished. He continued to Elisabeth Congdon's second-floor bedroom. Upon entering, he smothered the elderly woman with a pillow. Although she put up a struggle, Elisabeth eventually suffocated to death.

In an unexpected twist, investigators turned their suspicions toward Elisabeth's daughter Marjorie and her husband, Roger Caldwell. Evidence pointed to Roger as the man who committed the crimes. He was arrested, convicted and eventually admitted to the murders.

Many also speculated that Marjorie was the mastermind behind the plot and that a sizeable inheritance was her motive. The accusations were without proof though, and while later legal troubles landed the woman in prison, she was never convicted of any wrongdoing in the Congdon-Pietila murders.

Those were the facts as Tracy knew them, and she had become an expert at deflecting guests' questions about the crimes. The only thing she discussed with them less than the murders was the ghost. But that didn't keep employees from gossiping amongst themselves.

A few weeks earlier, a coworker had told Tracy the latest eerie tale. "I saw a flash of light at the top of the stairs," said her colleague. "I was about to remind the person that pictures aren't allowed inside, but when I looked again, no one was there."

Others claimed that Elisabeth's spirit resided within a doll inside the mansion. Reportedly, if one stared into the doll's eyes, he would see Elisabeth's ghost. Tracy wasn't sure which doll that might be. The story, while interesting, seemed a bit far-fetched to her.

She gave much more credence to some of the other accounts, especially those given by countless tourists. Many had claimed that the stairwell—the spot where Pietila was murdered—caused them to become light-headed. Dozens of others reported seeing Elisabeth's ghost standing at her bedroom window. Rumor had it that a few people even captured the apparition's image while photographing the mansion from the courtyard, although Tracy had never seen such a picture.

The basement, too, was a source of numerous tales. Even Tracy didn't like going down there; it "creeped her out." Of course, maybe it had something to do with the shadowy figure that supposedly roamed the mansion's bottom level.

However, the event that truly convinced Tracy of Glensheen's paranormal presence was experienced by Rick, her coworker and close friend. A matter-of-fact and down-to-earth kind of person, Rick was not prone to exaggeration and certainly would not find humor in making up a ghost story. That was why Tracy believed him completely.

Rick had been working high upon a ladder one afternoon, polishing one of the mansion's decorative chandeliers. His attention was focused on the work above him, and he believed himself to be alone.

Suddenly, he felt a hand clasp one of his ankles and tug at it. The yank was without much force, but the surprise of it almost sent Rick tumbling to the floor.

He braced himself against the ladder. Then, with his balance regained, he angrily looked downward at the person who had almost killed him. "What in the world are you—"

He stopped. No one else was there.

The fright was enough to send Rick home for the day—and the moment quickly became one of Glensheen's most notorious ghostly encounters.

As for Tracy, she had yet to experience anything more than the occasional cold spot or dark shadow seen in the corner of her eye. But after hearing Rick's chilling account, she wouldn't be climbing ladders at Glensheen Mansion any time soon—or ever.

Homemade Pizza

THERESA BANNING MISSED her father. He'd passed away just a few short weeks ago, and while she still had her mother and her younger sister, Carol, the Wadena home seemed much lonelier without Dad.

There was certainly no "bright side" to losing him, but as the Bannings gathered around the kitchen oven, smelling their homemade pizza, they joked anyway.

"Finally, we can have it again," Theresa's mother said in jest.

Theresa giggled, remembering the last time they had attempted to eat pizza in their home. She and Carol had bought a frozen pizza from the local grocery store, knowing full well that their father hated not only the taste of it but also its appearance and its smell.

After the girls had baked it, taken it out of the oven and set it on the counter to cool, their dad caught wind of the sinister scheme. He stormed into the kitchen. "What's this?" he shouted. Then, without waiting for an answer, he grabbed the freshly baked pizza and flung it out the kitchen door, into the backyard.

That had been nearly six years ago. The Bannings hadn't eaten pizza together since.

But now, finally, Carol cracked open the oven door and peeked inside. "It's done," she announced, grabbing two oven mitts and sliding them onto her hands.

She pulled the door all of the way open; it creaked loudly. Carol gently reached inside and lifted out their golden brown dinner. She smiled as she held up the pizza for her mother and sister to see.

Theresa's mouth instantly began to water. "It looks delicious," she said.

She was eager to taste her first homemade pizza in years, but she was also a bit melancholy. This would have been a violation of her father's wishes, had he still been alive. The fact that they were about to eat it was yet another reminder that her dad was—

The pizza flipped upward. (And so did the pan it had cooked upon.) It was as if someone slapped it hard from underneath, catapulting the food into the air!

It moved almost in slow motion. Theresa watched

the pizza fly for a moment, spinning end over end, before it sank to the floor, landing upside down with a dull splat.

The Bannings stared at it, their mouths agape.

"I— I didn't do it," Carol whispered. "Something knocked it out of my hands."

Theresa silently nodded; she already knew as much. Even if she had not seen the pan lift out of her sister's stationary hands, she would have known—for in that instant before their pizza was ruined, Theresa had sensed him again. Dad was back, if only for a second.

Theresa looked at her mother, and she looked at her sister. "I guess we're still not allowed to eat pizza," she declared, smiling more widely than she had in weeks.

Bedeviled Businesses

and Public Places

"Most people who went about saying
a ghost had poked them with a brolly
would be locked up somewhere."

–Pamela Stephenson

Worked to Death?

LINDA MOODY WAS ALMOST always the last person to leave the warehouse complex. As administrative assistant of the Bemidji building's second-story offices, Linda's final task each day was to walk up and down the hallway, ensuring that the offices were empty. Because the warehouse was filled with valuables, Linda's employer considered this daily walkthrough to be of the utmost importance and told her so on countless occasions. Thus, every night before five o'clock, Linda strolled down the long corridor, peeking into every room and even checking the men's and women's bathrooms. Once certain the floor was empty, she would shut off the lights and lock the doors on her way out.

Linda's coworkers usually left by 4:30 every day, leaving her alone in the building for a full 30 minutes, waiting for any end-of-day phone calls or last-minute deliveries. Yet despite the isolation (or perhaps because of it) Linda often heard what could only be described as "office sounds." Desk chairs squeaked, keyboards clattered, and computer mouses clicked.

Of course, to Linda, they were just noises, echoes of sounds heard all day, every day; she didn't pay much attention to them. And on the occasions when she was not the last to leave, when a coworker reported hearing those same peculiar noises, she shrugged it off as silliness or reasoned that someone else must have been in the offices with them. Linda wasn't about to consider the idea of ghosts. She was a rational, logical person, and ghost stories were, well, stories. It was going to take irrefutable proof to convince her otherwise.

That proof came on June 23, 2005.

As was her daily routine, Linda powered off her computer at about 4:50. On this day, the offices seemed unusually quiet. There weren't any phantom sounds of chairs moving or computer stations being used. For the first time in as long as Linda could remember, the offices actually felt empty.

The administrative assistant stood and began her long walk down the hallway, peeking into every room. It was one of those rare days in which her coworkers all remembered to turn off their computers and to shut off their lights. When Linda reached the far end of the hallway, she checked both bathrooms. As expected, she was completely alone.

It wasn't yet five o'clock, but Linda looked out the window and saw her husband drive into the parking lot. Deciding that 4:57 was close enough, Linda turned off the last of the office lights. She set the security alarm and locked the door. She jogged down the warehouse stairs and exited through the building's main entrance, which automatically locked behind her.

Linda hopped into the passenger seat of her husband Rick's old, beat-up truck.

"Not the last one today, huh?" he said.

She looked at him bewildered. "What?"

"I said, 'You're not the last one today.' You know, up there?" He gestured toward the second-floor offices.

"Yeah, I was," she replied, not quite getting the joke. Then, just to emphasize her point, she added, "I checked before I locked up."

Rick smiled. "Oh, really? I called you a second ago. The guy who answered told me you were coming down."

Linda felt the blood rush from her face. She stared at her husband, her mouth hanging open.

Rick's playful grin morphed into an expression of deep concern. "Are you okay?" he asked. "You look like you've seen a ghost."

"There can't be anyone up there. I checked every room. The lights are off. I set the alarm."

Her husband quickly double-checked his cell phone; Linda's extension was the last number dialed. "This is too weird," he admitted.

Against her better judgment but feeling obligated to do so, Linda returned—with Rick—inside the building. Upon further investigation, she found everything as she had left it. The offices were empty.

Rick looked at her, dumbfounded. "I don't get it. It doesn't make sense."

"Let's get out of here," was his wife's only response. Rick eagerly complied.

The next day, Linda reported the strange incident to her bosses. Management promised to look into it, and they were true to their word. But their efforts ended without any conclusive findings.

Linda became increasingly uncomfortable working in the warehouse offices—especially at the end of each day, when she was alone. In a matter of weeks, she was no longer with the company.

Today, no one will find any office workers inside that warehouse. They moved to a new location, although the company claims it was for unrelated reasons. Linda is happily employed at a new, ghost-free job. But as for the spirit that caused her to leave, one can only assume it still roams that office hallway, working a graveyard shift that never ends.

The Hanged Man

GUILTY. THAT ONE LITTLE WORD sealed John Moshik's fate. He had been accused of shooting another man in the back—murdering him—during a robbery that netted Moshik a watch and $14. The facts of the case were indisputable; his trial in Minneapolis City Hall's Chapel Courtroom proved it. But Moshik hoped his plea of "inherited insanity" might allow him to escape death.

It did not. Moshik's verdict meant the end of his life. At 3:35 a.m. on March 18, 1898, Moshik was hanged in the attic level of city hall's South Tower.

It was a gruesome scene, as Moshik's death was not quick. The job was botched; the convicted murderer hung squirming and writhing at the end of a noose—his arms and legs bound—for more than three minutes before death finally came.

Almost immediately thereafter, rumors began to swirl. Many believed the torture that Moshik endured unleashed his spirit upon city hall, and perhaps there was some truth behind the gossip. From custodians to visitors to lawyers and even judges, nearly everyone who entered the castle-like building seemed affected by the paranormal phenomena. Claims such as "I was chased by eerie footsteps" and "I saw a ghost" were heard countless times over the next several decades.

The Chapel Courtroom gained such a "haunted" reputation that, during a 1950s renovation project, it was removed from the plans. However, that didn't deter city hall's specter in the least.

The South Tower, where John Moshik had been executed, became known for its ghostly sightings and for the inexplicable sounds of flushing toilets. The mayor's adjacent office was also a prime target of the hanged man's ghost. Time and again, the artwork inside was rearranged—not just taken down but actually shuffled to different spots.

If that weren't enough, there were the all too common fifth-floor occurrences, most heavily concentrated near the locked stairwell that led to the South Tower . . .

"I'm telling you, I saw it!" the inmate declared.

Under different circumstances, Deputy Rex Stevens would've ignored the complaint. But he'd been working at the Hennepin County Adult Detention Center, on the fifth floor of Minneapolis City Hall, long enough to know better—even if the inmate sounded insane.

"There was a man wearing boxer shorts and nothing else," the inmate continued. "I was in the common room, and he stared at me through the window. Only he didn't look so much like a man. He was gray and faded. He looked like a ghost!"

Deputy Stevens nodded. He knew the rumors about this place, and he'd heard the stories. He'd even walked through a few cold spots and glimpsed an occasional spooky shadow, himself. But to actually see the dead eyes of a phantom, it was almost unbelievable.

Almost.

The problem was that Deputy Stevens had already heard this account five different times from five different inmates. And whenever that many sources told the same tale—believable or otherwise—it was worth checking out. But how did one investigate such a thing?

The video monitors were a logical first step. They yielded no visual evidence. Did that disprove the ghost stories? Not to Deputy Stevens' satisfaction. Of course, as he admitted to himself, ghostly tales weren't generally the sort of thing one proved or disproved. People either believed them or they didn't. Strangely though, while the deputy considered himself something of a skeptic, he couldn't bring himself to categorize the spirit of John Moshik as "nonsense." Perhaps he'd been working there too long and perhaps the place's ghostly lore was finally getting to him, but his instincts told him something supernatural was happening here.

His instincts were right. As Deputy Stevens hurried down the corridor, he walked through a spot so cold that it caused him to shiver.

He spun on his heels, turning back toward the temperature anomaly. For the briefest of instants, he saw it: a gray, faded man wearing nothing more than boxers. But then, as quickly as it appeared, the specter vanished.

Deputy Stevens' investigation was over.

Miners: Beware

CLINTON HARRIS WASN'T even supposed to be there. The shift's scheduled skip-tender was sick, and Harris had agreed to fill in. He couldn't afford to turn down the extra hours. So on this fifth day of February, 1924, he found himself at the bottom level of the Milford Manganese Mine's 200-foot shaft, just north of Crosby in central Minnesota. Harris operated the skip that hoisted ore out of the mine carts and dumped it into a bucket, where it was lifted to the surface. He never could have guessed that on this frigid winter afternoon tragedy was about to strike.

In recent months, despite the danger, the bottom level of the shaft had been dug closer and closer to neighboring Foley Lake; the manganese supply seemed richest there. Many miners sensed the impending danger and quit. Those who stayed learned their fateful mistake at 3:25 p.m. on that disastrous day—when the bottom level collapsed.

The cave-in unleashed a gust of wind so strong that it knocked out the electric lights throughout the mine, plunging the entire underground structure into darkness. This was only the beginning of the trouble, though. Above the shaft, a bog near Foley Lake suddenly broke through, flooding the mine in minutes. Many men at the bottom shaft were killed instantly, as the water pressure drove them into the walls with the force of a car wreck. Harris survived this first wave of danger, and in the moments when he initially recognized the crisis, he had an opportunity to escape. Heroically, he chose to stay behind to help his coworkers.

"We need to get out of here," another miner yelled. "Run for it!"

"I can't leave," Harris answered. "Someone has to warn the others." He hurried to the warning whistle and pulled. The high-pitched squeal wailed from above the mine, signaling trouble to the workers below.

The water level quickly rose around Harris, and he knew his demise was just seconds away. To ensure that his fellow miners received the signal even after his death, he tied himself to the whistle's pull string.

It was a noble sacrifice, but Harris couldn't have guessed that Milford Mine would flood so quickly. Only seven of the 48 men working escaped with their lives. The other 41 miners were trapped and killed in a mixture of mud and freezing water.

In the aftermath of what was to be the Iron Range's worst mining disaster on record, crews worked for nine months to retrieve the victims' bodies. But shortly thereafter, the mine was cleaned out and stabilized enough to reopen. Surprisingly, even this terrible disaster wouldn't deter Minnesota's crop of hardworking miners. Many men signed on to work, and Milford Mine was once again up and running.

The first to enter found their work environment almost unbearable. They were greeted by the stench of death and decay. That, however, was nothing compared to what the men saw.

They descended into the darkness of the 200-foot shaft, stifling their gags. As they neared the bottom level, their lamp light caught movement below.

"Hold it," said one of the men. "There might be something down there."

They all stopped and shone their lights downward. Their lamps revealed a most unexpected horror: the decomposed, barely recognizable figure of Clinton Harris! His apparition clung to the ladder, peering up at them (although his eye sockets were empty), toward the surface he never reached. The whistle cord hung from his waist.

Suddenly, to the men's continued terror, the mine's old whistle screamed to life, an ominous warning for the workers to leave—one made even more frightful by the fact that the whistle had been removed earlier, as had Harris's body.

No less than twelve miners bore witness to that supernatural sighting. All of them retreated out of the shaft at once, and none ever dared to re-enter Milford Mine. As for Harris's ghost, it must have been satisfied that its message was received. The specter was neither seen nor heard from again.

Wedding Crashers

IT WASN'T USUALLY this quiet, this early. The Wabasha Street Speakeasy should have roared with the party sounds of big band music, drinking and dancing. But this was the early 1930s, and gangsters pretty much ran the place—they called the shots.

Ever since alcohol had been declared illegal in 1920, police who tried enforcing the law couldn't keep up with the criminals eager to break it. To make matters worse, Saint Paul police chief John O'Connor declared that such outlaws were free from persecution in his jurisdiction, as long as they behaved themselves while within the city limits. Saint Paul—and the Wabasha Street Caves in particular—became a known hangout for gangsters.

The underground sandstone caves provided plenty of privacy for the lawbreakers and the city's "thirsty" citizens. Notorious criminals including John Dillinger, Babyface Nelson and Pretty Boy Floyd mingled with the rest of the population, while the liquor that so much of the public craved was provided. The gangsters, though outlaws, were likeable, famous and rich.

So on this night, as four known criminals indulged in a private game of poker and as a fifth asked the band to call it quits—even though it was well before midnight—the band stopped playing, the taps ran dry, and the speakeasy cleared out.

The only person remaining with the five men was a waitress, charged with the task of closing the nightclub as soon as the gangsters had finished their game. She was working in the kitchen when she heard the gunshots.

The waitress ran to the Fireside Room, where the men had been. She found three of the gangsters dead; the other two were gone.

The young woman called the police, summoning several uniformed officers. They took her statement and left her while they examined the scene of the crime. But much to the waitress's surprise, the officers returned almost two hours later to accuse her of making a false report. Apparently, the cover-up was on.

Outraged, the girl stormed into the Fireside Room; it appeared completely normal! The bodies had been moved, the blood mopped, the chairs straightened. But while the crooked cops had been able to clean the room, there was little they could do about the bullet holes in the walls.

Nevertheless, the crime went ignored. The victims' bodies—buried somewhere within the Wabasha Street Caves—were never found.

Jane Holloway knew the caves' history, especially the seedy parts. She was also aware of the ghost stories. Strange glowing orbs, phantom music, dark and spooky shadows—she'd heard them all. Her personal favorite came from the 1970s, when the caves served as a disco dance hall. The manager and one of his employees were startled by the appearance of a rather angry patron. The stranger barrelled toward them, dressed as a 1930s gangster, causing the two workers to scatter. However, the charging man didn't veer in either direction. He continued forward, disappearing through the wall.

Yes, it was a pretty good tale, and there were dozens more where that came from. None of it bothered Jane. What mattered most to her was the fact that the Wabasha Street Caves made a perfectly beautiful, perfectly unique location for a wedding reception.

The blessed event did not disappoint. It was exactly as the bride dreamed it would be, right down to every last detail: the salmon dinner, the wedding party toasts, the cutting of the cake, the first dance, Jane would not change a second of it.

She was also pleasantly surprised that her nephew Charlie got into the "spirit" of the evening. Before the eight-year-old left with his family, he hugged Jane.

"I'm glad you could come, Charlie. What was your favorite part of tonight?" the bride asked.

He smiled and innocently replied, "Playing with the gangster men."

Jane laughed out loud and hugged him again. She never would've guessed that even her youngest relative was aware of the caves' ghostly reputation.

However, she didn't laugh when she returned from her honeymoon and saw the reception pictures. In a particularly memorable shot, Charlie sat at a table, grinning widely, surrounded by several blurred and misty forms—each of which bore a striking similarity to the shape of man.

Charlie's funny joke had been no joke at all.

Ghost Writer

SHE WAS A LITTLE BIT SCARED. And excited. Moving to Concordia College in Moorhead, across the state from her hometown outside the Twin Cities, was the hardest thing Lora Lemke had ever done. It was the beginning of a new life for the 1994 Elk River graduate. In her first 24 hours of college, she had already made a few friends, but she also missed her home, her own bed and of course her mom and dad.

To make matters worse, Lora had been assigned a room on the fifth floor of Hoyum Hall—a floor that, she had come to learn, was haunted. According to the gossip already passed among the hall's population, a student had killed herself there years ago. The details varied. Some said she hung herself. Others believed she jumped out of a window. But everyone seemed to agree that her spirit remained on the premises.

Lora's dorm room, which she shared with another freshman, Sarah, lay at the heart of these ghostly tales, for it was in their room that the suicidal student had apparently lived—and died. And it was in their room that most of the paranormal phenomena occurred.

Eerie Electronics

For Lora and Sarah, the haunting began innocuously enough. The two students sat in their room studying late one afternoon. At her desk, Lora concentrated on the textbook in front of her.

Beep!

The noise startled the room's two occupants. It was followed by the muffled, recorded sound of Lora's own voice. "Hello, you've reached Lora and Sarah. We can't come to the phone right now. Please leave a message." Another beep. Then nothing.

Lora glanced over her shoulder. Sarah met her gaze. The two shared a shrug and returned to their studies. It was the first of many similar instances in which the answering machine inexplicably activated.

With each passing week, the girls' electronics acted odder and odder. Most of the abnormalities occurred while Lora and Sarah slept. Almost weekly, the duo was awakened in the middle of the night by their lights being clicked on. Naturally, the roommates first suspected a prankster as the culprit. However, even after they took to locking their door, the phenomena continued.

More troubling to Lora was the erratic behavior of her alarm clock. By her own admission, Lora had a hint of obsessive compulsiveness in her. She checked and double-checked her alarm settings every night. Yet, despite that, her clock buzzed to life at unexpected times: in the darkness of night, in the middle of the day and sometimes mere minutes before it was supposed to. Each time, Lora rechecked the settings, and each time the alarm schedule remained as it should have. So why, then, did her alarm clock work so inconsistently? She may have chalked it up to a faulty machine, except her roommate's clock did the very same thing.

Perhaps one might have been able to find rational explanations for these occurrences—electrical surges or some such—but this was only the beginning.

Bizarre happenings surfaced in the fifth floor bathrooms. Several girls, on multiple occasions, entered the otherwise empty bathroom area to find all of the water running, every sink and every shower. The faucets had been turned on without cause or reason.

Strange Bedfellow
By Thanksgiving, the entire hall was abuzz about the paranormal activity. However, the school year's two most bizarre moments had yet to occur.

The first came on a frigid Moorhead night in early December. It was well after 10 p.m., and the hallway was empty. Most residents were off hanging out with friends or in their rooms studying. Lora and Sarah's neighbor, Suzie, was alone next door, winding down after a long day of classes and work. She relaxed on her bed, listening to music through her headphones, eyes closed.

When she sensed someone enter the dorm room, she didn't think twice about it. And when someone laid down beside her, she didn't bother opening her eyes. She was, after all, a freshman at Concordia College. By this time of year, her floormates were like sisters. It was common practice for them to pop into each others' rooms, just for the comfort of being near a kindred spirit.

Whoever it is, Suzie began to wonder, *she sure is squirmy.* The student opened her eyes. No one was there!

Suzie's hands muffled her scream. She leapt out of bed and dashed next door to Lora and Sarah's room. She stayed with them, refusing to return to bed until her roommate arrived nearly two hours later.

The Letter

As the first semester wound down, Lora's history class quite literally kept her up at night. She had gotten into the habit of doing her homework in the study room down the hall, allowing Sarah to sleep in peace. Lora typed away on her word processor—a machine halfway between a typewriter and a computer—frantically trying to finish a report that was due in a matter of hours.

As she typed her last sentence, she glanced at the clock. It was after 1 a.m. Lora saved her document and rubbed her eyes as she powered down the machine. She unplugged it, exhaled an exhausted sigh and lugged the word processor back to her room. She set it on her desk, and she fell into bed. She was asleep almost before her head hit the pillow.

When Lora awakened the next morning, Sarah was still in bed. Lora had already overslept, and she needed her report. She plugged the word processor into the wall, but as her machine came to life, she saw what in that instant may have been the worst horror she could have imagined: an error message.

Lora felt a surge of panic. Had her report been erased by an electrical glitch? She scrambled to find out. Her processor's message instructed her to press "return" to get back to the main menu. Lora hastily did so. But curiously, instead of bringing her to that all-too-familiar page, something entirely different popped onto the tiny viewing screen: a letter, one that chilled Lora to her core.

The letter (which appears in its entirety on page 111) was written, as if to two high school friends, about the goings-on of a college freshman. Strangely, it was an amalgam of Lora's and Sarah's lives, but it referenced people whom neither of them knew.

For a moment, Lora entertained the idea that her roommate was pranking her, but practical jokes were not in Sarah's nature. Besides, it would've meant that Sarah had awakened in the middle of the night, plugged in the machine, powered it on, typed the eerie message, shut everything down, then returned to bed—all without waking Lora. That seemed unlikely.

A short conversation and Sarah's sincere shock upon reading the letter confirmed it: This was no joke. They had just received a note from a ghost.

Urban Legend

The rest of the school year passed without anything more than the "usual" ghostly occurrences. Needless to say, both Lora and Sarah moved to different dormitories as sophomores.

Years later, when Lora worked as a senior advisor for incoming freshmen, she was delighted to hear one of the eighteen-year-olds ask, "Have you ever heard about the Hoyum girl who got a letter from a ghost?"

Lora laughed heartily and answered with pride. "I haven't just heard it. That girl was me!"

Childhood Chillers

"The past is a ghost, the future a
dream, and all we ever have is now."

—Bill Cosby

The Graves of Annie Mary

IMAGINE A DAY like any other. You've spent your allotted time working. You've finished all that needed doing. At long last, it's time for some fun. You choose a favorite activity, one you've enjoyed countless times before. You laugh. You play. All is well in the world—until something goes terribly wrong.

You slip. You fall. You black out.

Imagine opening your eyes, only you're not entirely sure they're open. You're lying on your back, surrounded by a darkness you've never experienced before.

You sit up, or at least you try. You hit your head

before moving more than a few inches. You quickly bring up your hands. They scrape the wooden barrier above you. You're trapped inside a tiny box, and you are completely alone.

Now imagine you're six years old.

So began one of the most tragic, most disturbing ghostly tales in Minnesota history. The year was 1886. Richard and Lizzie Twente lived on a farm in southwestern Minnesota's Albin Township (south of Sleepy Eye) with their five children, including Annie Mary.

For the sweet, six-year-old girl, October 24 began as a typical day. Unfortunately, it became anything but normal when Annie Mary fell from a hayloft and slipped into a coma.

Her father was not a model parent. In fact, Richard was known by neighbors for his fits of rage and his "unstable" mental condition. One of his most notorious acts of insanity occurred on a cold winter day. Richard became consumed by the notion that his family was in danger—although from what no one knows. He forced his family onto a sled and trekked across the prairie with no destination in mind. It is likely that they all would have frozen to death if Lizzie had not convinced her husband to return home.

Given Richard's reckless behavior, it came as little surprise that, upon discovering his unconscious daughter, he did not consult a physician.

"She's dying," he declared wildly. "Lung fever is going to take my little girl from me!"

Two days later, on October 26, Richard pronounced Annie Mary dead. He buried her at Iberia Cemetery.

What happened next is uncertain. Many believe Lizzie was plagued by nightmares. Others claim Richard feared that grave robbers would steal his daughter's body. Regardless of the reason, the Twente family dug up Annie Mary's body, and what they reportedly found was the most ghastly of horrors.

The coffin's interior was riddled with scratch marks. Annie Mary's fingernails were bloody. Torn chunks of hair were clenched inside her fists. The little girl's face was a mask of terror. She had been buried alive, and the ordeal had killed her.

The Twentes were overwhelmed with grief (so much so that Richard was eventually committed to the state hospital in Saint Peter). They moved their daughter's body to a new gravesite, one that overlooked their farm and the adjacent road from atop a nearby hill.

Richard built a wooden fence around Annie Mary's burial plot to protect her from evils known only to him. Later, he decided that the wooden fence wasn't enough. In its place, he built a stone wall and added a locked iron gate at its opening.

As legend has it, the wall and its gate may have kept unwanted visitors out, but they could not keep Annie Mary's spirit within.

"Look at that," said a man traveling on horseback. He gestured toward the hillside. The ghostly figure of a child stood, staring at him, her white dress shining.

The man's horse reared. His companion's did the same. Despite their most vigorous coaxings, the animals refused to venture any closer to Annie Mary's grave. The two travelers were forced to find an alternate route.

It was an encounter rumored to have repeated itself dozens of times with any number of different riders, for it was said that animals could sense the poor girl's spirit. No beast would willingly venture near her gravesite.

Similarly, in later years, motorists often experienced car troubles as they passed the mysterious location. Headlights failed, and vehicles inexplicably stalled.

For more than a century, Annie Mary haunted that hillside and its surrounding areas. However, time was not kind to her resting place. The walls became cracked and damaged. Her tombstone was uprooted from its base. The gate was removed completely. Worse yet, Annie Mary's gravesite was a frequent target of vandals. Over the years, far too many teenagers trespassed upon the property, and many of them dug into the ground or stole pieces of the stone monument built by Annie Mary's father.

At last, in 1996, the girl's body and presumably her spirit were finally put to rest. Her remains were disinterred, and Annie Mary was buried for the third time. Today, she lies next to her parents at a cemetery in northern Minnesota.

As for her hilltop monument, that too is gone. The stone wall was demolished, the trees were cut down, and the land was planted over.

Those who live near Albin Township know this story well, and they will not soon forget the infamous location of Annie Mary's burial plot. However, they are grateful—as we all should be—that, after more than a hundred years and three burials, Annie Mary finally found peace.

Demon Doll

LIKE MOST OF US, the Jones family equated the word "haunting" with a scary building—a place in which the unexplainable occurred. Lights flickered. Furniture moved. Eerie noises were heard.

They didn't know that hauntings also took another form. Ghosts weren't always confined to homes, barns or hillsides. Instead, they sometimes attached themselves to objects (or "totems"). These spirits were free to roam wherever their totems went: a car, a store, an office. And sadly—as Kate and Emily Jones discovered—there was just one way to get rid of such specters.

It was Christmas in Mora, 1997, and the Jones girls knew what they wanted: a My Height Fashion Doll. Every trip to the local store inevitably ended with their mom, Angie, being dragged to the toy aisle, so she could see yet again this most coveted of gifts.

"Please," the girls would beg.

"We'll see," Angie always countered.

The doll was expensive—too expensive, in fact. But a few months earlier, Angie had hit the jackpot, or so she thought. She'd come across a used My Height Fashion Doll at a garage sale, and she had purchased it in a "grab bag" (one that also included tattered, ragged children's clothes). Now, the doll was safely hidden inside her bedroom closet.

That magical Christmas Day finally arrived, and Kate and Emily devoured their presents like a pack of hungry wolves. When Angie unveiled the My Height Fashion Doll for the grand finale, Kate and Emily erupted with glee.

Unfortunately, their joy didn't last.

Over the course of the next several days, the girls began finding the toy in unusual places—spots they were certain they hadn't left it. Somehow, the toy wound up in their parents' bed, in the bathroom, beneath the dining room table and even in their mom's car.

On New Year's Eve, Kate and Emily brought the doll to their cousin Amanda's house. They told her all about the possessed toy, and the trio decided to conduct an experiment. Before they went to bed, the girls sat the doll on a chair in Amanda's room. Each promised not to touch it, and then—one by one—they fell asleep.

Kate and Emily awakened the next morning to the sound of Amanda's scream. The girls bolted upright in their sleeping bags. Then they screamed too.

The doll was still sitting in the chair, but its head was turned backward.

The girls' parents burst into the room, but after the children frantically explained, most of the adults didn't believe them. They scratched their heads, shrugged their shoulders and said things like, "Those kids and their imaginations," and, "How do they come up with it?"

Angie, however, wasn't convinced that her children were telling a tall tale. Later that day, when her family arrived back at their Mora home, Angie sat down with Kate and Emily for a serious talk.

"I want you to tell me the truth," said Angie. "Did one of you do that to the doll?"

"No," the girls proclaimed.

"Do you promise you didn't?" Angie asked.

"I promise," each of them replied.

"Then let's try one more experiment," said Angie.

They put the doll in Angie's bedroom closet, and each agreed to leave it there for a week—just to see if anything strange might happen.

They didn't wait long.

The next morning, Kate awakened to the scare of her life. The My Height Fashion Doll wasn't in her mom's closet anymore; it was in bed with her!

This final ghostly encounter left the Joneses with a decision to make; it proved to be a surprisingly difficult one. Despite the scares the doll had caused, the girls were reluctant to give up this most precious of Christmas gifts. Angie, too, did not want to discard such a memorable present. But in the end, the family chose to remove the toy—and its spirit—from their home. They broke off the doll's head, arms and legs, and they threw the toy out with the rest of their trash.

January 2, 1998, marked the final day in which the Jones family experienced a paranormal encounter. It would seem that, in getting rid of the toy, they also expelled the ghost. If only all hauntings could be ended so easily.

Imaginary Friend

ALISA SCHROM STOOD outside her daughter Michelle's bedroom, listening.

"What did your daddy do?" asked the three-year-old child. She waited a moment and then said, "What's a postmaster general?" She paused. "Oh, a mailman. Why didn't you say so?"

Alisa marveled at her daughter's imagination. The pacing was perfect. It was almost as if she were having a real conversation with her dolls—or imaginary friend.

"I'm sorry," said Michelle sympathetically. "I don't like being sick either."

Alisa smiled and started downstairs, but then her daughter said something that surprised her.

"Wow, a real elevator? In here?"

The pieces of the pretend dialogue suddenly fell into place. Alisa recalled an actual conversation she'd shared with their elderly neighbor months earlier. He informed her that the Schroms' Austin home had been built in 1933—complete with a working elevator that ran from the basement to the second floor. The house was owned by the town's postmaster general, and as Alisa's neighbor told it, the postmaster's young daughter grew gravely ill. His poor child suffered at home for days, feverish and bedridden. Eventually, the disease (the elderly gentleman could not remember what it was) took her life; the girl died under the Schroms' very roof.

Strange, thought Alisa. *I wouldn't expect Michelle to remember all of those details. In fact, I don't remember her being there when I learned them.* She shrugged, chalking it up to the power of the toddler mind.

The coming days brought similar "conversations." Michelle would be in her bedroom, and Alisa would overhear the girl's one-sided chat with her imaginary friend. Finally, Alisa's curiosity got the better of her.

"Who are you talking to?" she asked her daughter.

"The little girl," Michelle replied, matter-of-factly.

"What little girl?" said Alisa.

"The little girl that lives here, but she's gone now."

Alisa's suspicions were confirmed: Her daughter had an imaginary friend.

As another few weeks passed, Alisa thought nothing of those private, whispered talks behind Michelle's bedroom door. But when her daughter started playing inside Alisa's bedroom, the woman took exception. She stepped upstairs late one afternoon, on her way to the bathroom, and she heard Michelle jumping on her bed.

She peeked into her room, and she spied the child's flowing, brownish hair and a long, white dress bouncing up and down. "Stop that," she ordered as she breezed past the doorway and into the bathroom.

Michelle peeked inside, looking as innocent as ever. "Stop what, Mommy?"

Alisa frowned. "Please don't jump on my bed."

"I wasn't on your bed," Michelle protested. "I was in my room."

Alisa tried not to roll her eyes. Her sweet little girl was learning to lie.

Two days later, Alisa again heard Michelle jumping on the bed. Her daughter had been warned; this time there would be trouble.

The irritated mother stomped up the stairs and stormed to her bedroom. Michelle would be caught red-handed; she would not be able to lie this time. However, as Alisa neared the door, she heard her daughter's voice.

"Get off Mommy's bed," said the child. "She doesn't like jumping."

Alisa's anger was replaced by curiosity. She stopped herself from bursting inside and instead peeked around the corner.

She once again saw the flowing, brownish hair and the long, white dress bounding atop her bed.

And then she saw her daughter.

Michelle stood at the foot of the bed, ordering her imaginary friend to stop. Only it wasn't an imaginary friend, was it?

Alisa nearly fell backward and down the stairs behind her. The woman's startled gasp was so loud and forceful that it caused Michelle to flinch—and Michelle's ghostly companion to vanish.

A few hours later, when Alisa had gathered enough nerve, she returned to her room alone and sat on her bed. "I hope you can hear me," she announced. "I'm Michelle's mom. I want you to know it's all right if you play with my daughter, but please stop jumping on my bed. And if possible, I don't want to see you again. You about gave me a heart attack!"

The spirit of the little girl must have taken note of the message. After that day, Alisa's requests were granted.

Michelle continued talking to her ghostly friend in her bedroom, but as the years passed and as Michelle grew older, the conversations became rarer. Eventually, they ceased altogether.

Today, the Schroms are uncertain whether the phantom child still inhabits their home, as they've had no contact with her in years. They only hope that the little girl's spirit has found peace, wherever it may be.

The Man Upstairs

Editor's Note: Following is the author's personal account; it is told from his point of view.

THE HOUSE WAS OLD and abandoned. So, of course, my best friend Ryan Melby and I grew up day-dreaming about the mysteries and adventures that lay beyond its rotting, decrepit doors. After all, we were boys; we believed that any building which appeared so frightening from the outside must contain countless hidden terrors within.

The spooky-looking home rested at the edge of the Melby family's property, eight miles outside Pipestone in southwestern Minnesota. Ryan and I logged hundreds of hours buzzing by the old house on his motorbike, and we fantasized about sneaking inside, seeing a ghost and thereby discovering proof that such specters existed.

But by 1990, our motives had changed. We were both fifteen years old and hurrying to bridge the gap between youth and adulthood. Quashing our foolish beliefs in spirits and haunted places would bring us one step closer to the "grown-up" world.

So it was on a hot and humid August afternoon, with summer winding down and with another school year soon to begin, that Ryan and I decided to act. Finally, after all these years, we were going inside.

I waited for him to finish his chores, and then we started toward the old farmhouse together. But almost before we began, we crossed paths with Chris Rothen, the Melby family's nineteen-year-old farmhand. We must have been wearing guilty expressions because Chris asked suspiciously, "What are you doing?"

"Nothing," Ryan replied too quickly.

Chris looked at us, looked toward the old house and shook his head. He said nothing else as he continued on his way. We did the same, walking a little more quickly than before. By the time we reached our destination, we were more worried that Chris was going to tell on us than we were about ghouls and ghosts.

"Do you think the door will open?" I asked.

"I don't know," Ryan answered, sounding almost as nervous as I felt. "Why don't you check?"

I took hold of the screen door and pulled the handle. It resisted, as if warning us to stay out. But we wouldn't be denied. I gave the door three hard tugs, and it swung outward with a loud squeal. The door behind it opened without a fight, and we stepped inside.

We were greeted by the sight of an empty, gutted house, its skeletal frame exposed. It wasn't like all of those abandoned places in the movies. There weren't many cobwebs—but there was a lot of dust. There were also plenty of odds and ends scattered about the place: knickknacks, dishes and clothes.

Ryan and I weaved in and out of the many rooms, feeling braver with each step. Our need to stick together soon subsided. Ryan wandered further into the house, while I discovered stairs leading upward. By now, I was feeling invincible again—as only a teenager can—so I decided to take the stairs. I moved forward, one step, two steps, three steps.

As I reached the fourth step, I rounded a corner. I could suddenly see the openness of the second floor. I scanned the visible area above me, and the blood in my veins froze.

Just around the bend, at the top of the stairs, stood the figure of a heavyset man. The upper half of his body was obstructed from my view, but his thick legs and navy blue coveralls were unmistakable.

Two words flashed through my mind: *ghost* followed by *run*.

And that's what I did.

I stormed toward the exit, and I screamed, "Melby!"

I didn't bother looking behind me. I didn't bother opening that rickety screen door. I braced myself, and I launched into it. The door exploded—breaking into hundreds of scraps and splinters. I kept running.

Outside, Chris had been strolling over to check on us. When he saw me crash through the entrance, he sprinted the forty yards or so that separated us.

He reached me at nearly the same time as Ryan. But while Ryan yelled about getting in trouble, Chris looked me in the eyes and smiled. "You saw him, didn't you?"

Ryan stopped shouting. He stared at me, bemused.

I took a moment to catch my breath, nodded my head and muttered, "Yeah, I think so."

"Let's go see if he's still there," said Chris.

Curiosity got the better of me. I was already beginning to wonder if I had imagined the entire encounter. I led Chris and Ryan back inside and to the stairwell, but I wasn't about to go up.

The two of them pushed past me and strode up the steps. They stopped in almost exactly the same spot where I had spied the mysterious figure.

"What did you see?" Chris shouted.

I peeked up at him—only so I could answer his question. "It was a man. He was wearing blue coveralls."

Chris bent down, reached forward and pulled something off the floor. "You mean these?" He held in his hands the navy blue coveralls that, moments earlier, I had seen someone—or something—wearing.

My belief in ghosts was certainly not quashed on that day, and neither Ryan nor I ever ventured inside that house again. The dilapidated old structure is no longer there, but my memory of that paranormal encounter will stay with me for as long as I live.

Also Available

More Minnesota Ghost Stories

Ghostly Tales of Minnesota
33 stories • $7.95

The Mysterious North Shore
21 stories • $8.95

More Books by Ryan Jacobson

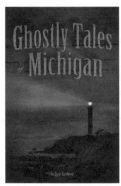

Ghostly Tales of Michigan
27 stories • $8.95

Ghostly Tales of Wisconsin
28 stories • $8.95

Selected Bibliography

American Hauntings. www.prairieghosts.com.
Troy Taylor. 2010.

Famous Crimes (The Minnesota Series). Sheri O'Meara
and Merle Minda. D Media Inc., Minneapolis: 2008.

Haunted America. Michael Norman and Beth Scott.
Tom Doherty Associates LLC, New York: 1994.

Haunted Houses. www.hauntedhouses.com.
Video Producers Inc. 2007.

Haunted Heartland. Beth Scott and Michael Norman.
Barnes & Noble Books, New York: 1985.

*Haunted Places: The National Directory: Ghostly Abodes,
Sacred Sites, UFO Landings and Other Supernatural
Locations.* Dennis William Hauck. Penguin Books,
New York: 2002.

"Milford Mine Disaster" Parts I–III: *NewsHopper*™.
Connie Pettersen. Brainerd, MN: March 11–25, 2006.

Minnesota Road Guide to Haunted Locations, The. Chad
Lewis and Terry Fisk. Unexplained Research
Publishing Company, Eau Claire, WI: 2005.

Shadowlands, The. http://theshadowlands.net.
Dave Juliano. 2010.

The Letter

Editor's Note: Following is the letter referenced in "Ghost Writer" (pages 84–89). It appears exactly as it was written.

DEAR BRITTNI AND JOEY,

How are you two doing? Getting excited for Christmas I'm sure. How is school Brittni? Are you learning lots? I hope so. And is gymnastics keeping you busy?

I am definitely keeping busy with homework; only 6 more days until I can come home; I can hardly wait!!! Then I'll have 17 days with no homework! I only wish I didn't have final exams to take. My religion and music theory ones are going to be hard; but I'll have two days to study, so that'll be nice. I spent all day today working on my final exam for history – it's taking forever.....

I was on a choir trip to Minneapolis on Wed, Thurs, and Fri. We performed two sold out shows for 2450 people each time at Orchestra Hall – it was so much fun to perform there!! I can't believe we've already performed six concerts and are all done!! Of course Thurs. morning we had 2½ hours to shop, so I liked that!

It's been really cold lately – I freeze walking to classes. I wish it weren't quite so windy!

My roommate and I exchanged Christmas presents today; that was fun. But now our little Christmas tree is pretty bare.

I just found out my cousin will be home from the Marines for christmas, so that will be lots fo fun to see him again. He hasn't been home for Christmas for 2 years!!

Last night Mona, Katie, Beth and I went shopping at the mall and then to a basketball game; unfortunately, then I had to come home to do homework.

Well, I'd better get back to my studying. Hopefully I'll see you over Christmas break! Have a good week at school. Say [end of letter]

About the Author

NEARLY TWENTY YEARS ago, Ryan Jacobson had a brush with the "unexplainable." Not long after, his older brother, Jason, introduced Ryan to his first horror novel. It was then that Ryan's love of reading ghost stories was born. He later turned his passion for books into a career as an author. He has written ten children's books and is also the author of *Ghostly Tales of Michigan* and *Ghostly Tales of Wisconsin*.

Ryan resides in Mora, Minnesota, with his wife Lora, sons Jonah and Lucas, and dog Boo. For more about the author, visit www.RyanJacobsonOnline.com.